Bumblebee Buzz

Melanie Richardson Dundy

> Narrative Non-fiction
> This book is researched and factual
> but narrated by a fictional character.

No part of this book may be reproduced
or transmitted in any form or by any means
without permission from the author.

ISBN: 978-1-0882-5829-3
copyright 2023
by Melanie Richardson Dundy

MDCT Publishing@gmail.com
melanie.dundy@icloud.com
website: ChildrensBooksByMelanie.com

Dedicated to Kristine Geier, and all the students lucky enough to have her for their teacher.

Did you know?

In Native American symbolism, the bumblebee represents honesty, pure thinking, willingness, and drive.

Did you also know?

The name Dumbledore from the Harry Potter series is an old word for bumblebee. Author JK Rowling chose the name because she imagined the wizard humming to himself as he went about his business.

This is a honeybee.
Honeybees make
delicious honey.

This is a wasp.
I have no idea
what it does.

And this is me.
I am a bumblebee. Bumblebees pollinate flowers and crops.

Hello

My name is Bumble. Bumble Bee, to be more specific. I don't like my first name. It was given to me by a bully, who said I clumsily bumbled around all over the place. And, sadly, I do bumble around on cold mornings. It's the way I warm up to be able to fly.

But when that bully saw me struggling one morning, he laughed at me and called me a bumbling bee. The bumble part stuck, not only to me but to all bees that look like me.

It's okay, though. We bumblebees have grown kind of fond of the name, and we are much too smart to let a bully bother us. We all know bullies are nincompoops who deserve no respect.

Moving on —

I am a pudgy, fuzzy insect with short stubby legs. I am typically black and yellow.

My body has 3 parts:

thorax

head

abdomen

I have 5 eyes (2 large eyes on either side of my head and 3 eyes on the top of my head).

I am so furry that sometimes I think I am a mammal. But I'm not. I am an insect.

I have 2 antennae, 6 jointed legs, and 2 stomachs. One stomach is for eating, and the other is for storing water or flower nectar that I carry back to my nest to eat and share with others.

My heart is so big, it runs down the entire length of my body. My blood does not travel through veins and arteries like yours does. My blood just sloshes around inside of me. Slosh, slosh.

Let me make one thing very, very clear —

I AM NOT A BUG.

I do not ever want you to confuse me or any bumblebee with a bug! We are insects!

If you don't believe me, just ask any entomologist who studies bumblebees.

It is true that all bugs are insects, BUT not all insects are bugs. Bugs have mouth parts that pierce other insects, animals, and plants to suck juice from them. UGH!

I do not have piercing mouth parts for sucking ANYTHING!

I am an insect!

What is un-bee-lievable (sorry, I couldn't resist) is that I can fly. There is nothing about me that is aerodynamic (shaped to allow me to move quickly through the air).

With my round, pudgy, little body, I shouldn't even be able to get off the ground!

Amazingly, though, I can fly. I can fly as fast as 10 miles an hour.

I do it by flapping my wings back and forth like a helicopter propeller instead of up and down like a bird.

I can flap my wings close to 200 times per second. That's about the same number of revolutions per minute as some motorcycle engines. Isn't that amazing?

I should go 'vroom, vroom' instead of 'buzz, buzz.'

I am so cool!

Okay, now I have a question for you.

I have a brain the size of a poppy seed, so do you think I can learn? Do you think I can think?

Here are some facts to help you make your decision:

1. A bumblebee must memorize the landscape and evaluate its flower options.

2. A garden of flowers that is full of nectar and pollen in the morning may be depleted just hours later by other pollinators. In that case, the bumblebee has to make quick decisions and change plans to survive.

3. Bumblebees like to play. We really do. When a group of entomologists gave some friends of mine little wooden balls, they started rolling them all over the place. It was clear that they were having a lot of fun.

There are three types of bumblebees in a colony.

1. The Queen is the most important bee in the nest. She is the mother of all the other bees in the colony.

2. The Worker Bee, like me, collects food, and maintains the nest.

3. The Drone is the only male in the colony and the only bee that has no stinger. Its eyes are twice as big as those of a worker bee. A drone's only job is to mate with the queen to produce offspring.

Queen　　　　　Worker Bee　　　　　Drone

DRONES

Let's start with the drones because the poor guys are so outnumbered by the females. The drones are the only males in the colony. Their only job is to mate with the queen to produce the next generation of bumblebees.

Once the drones have completed their one job, they are kicked out of the nest. They are not even allowed back in to sleep at night. None of the female bees show them any respect or show any interest in them at all. So, from then on, it's all play and no work for the drones. They can sit around playing video games all day if that's what they want to do. Sadly, though, drones don't live very long after they mate with the queen.

The queen and worker bees just want the drones out of their way so they can get on with the important work of creating and caring for the next generation of bumblebees.

Drones do not have stingers, and they also do not have the ability to gather nectar or pollen. Therefore, they are dependent on the worker bees to bring them food.

THE QUEEN BEE

As I mentioned earlier, the queen bee is the most important bee in the nest and is the mother to all the other bees. She is also the only bee in the colony that lives through the winter. The first thing she does after coming out of winter hibernation is find a location for a nest. She builds her nest and raises her young in very small spaces.

She likes to build her nest close to the ground or even under the ground. She might build the nest under a clump of grass, in an old bird's nest, or in a hollow tree. My queen built our nest in an empty mouse hole, which is great. It came with a soft, roll-around-comfy, fur lining.

The queen lays eggs that look like sausages, tiny, tiny sausages. She then builds a wax honey pot, which covers her eggs and often covers the entire nest.

The queen sits on her little sausage-shaped eggs for about two weeks. She shivers to warm up and keep her eggs nice and toasty warm.

If the nest gets too warm when the weather heats up, bumblebees have their own unique cooling system. Some of the worker bees hover over the nest and vibrate their wings like crazy — as fast as their little bodies allow. The bees perform as very efficient ceiling fans. The hotter it is, the more worker bees join in to hover.

Bumblebee colonies usually have between 50 and 500 bees. Can you believe honeybees have colonies of well over 50,000 bees?

The queen is able to determine the sex of the eggs, so she makes sure her first set of eggs are all female worker bees like me.

The queen only takes care of the first batch of babies. The new worker bees that come from that batch are responsible for the care of future babies.

After laying her first set of eggs, the only thing the queen is expected to do is lay and hatch new eggs over and over again. In fact, the queen usually lays another batch of eggs while the first batch is still developing.

When the little sausage-shaped eggs hatch, out pop the baby bees. They are called larvae, and sadly, the larvae look like little maggots. Poor little things.

When the larvae are two weeks old, they spin cocoons around themselves and stay cuddled up inside for 4 to 5 weeks until they are adults.

THE WORKER BEES

I've saved the best for last: ME. I am a worker bee. Now, you would think we worker bees, being female like the queen, could produce offspring of our own, but get this: The queen actually produces a hormone that stops all the other females in the nest from mating. That's her sneaky and effective way of keeping her elite position as queen bee.

Worker bees can still lay eggs, but the queen likes to gobble them up — again to maintain her supremacy. I'm sure you are probably thinking that the bumblebee world can be hard, especially for us worker bees, and you are right.

I, along with my fellow worker bees, do all the real work. My jobs are endless. I wait on the queen, clean and guard the nest, find food, feed the drones, and take care of the next batch of baby bees.
                    Whew!

Maybe, instead of being called a worker bee, I should be called a Cinderella bee with all the chores I have every day.

We bumblebees do not like rain. If I am out of the nest when rain starts to fall, I run for cover. If I am at home when it starts to rain, I stay home until the rain stops.

What I like even less than rain is getting caught outside the nest when the temperature suddenly drops. If that happens, I can lose my ability to fly.

Not being able to fly, I have to snuggle down under or inside a flower until morning. I hold my pollen close and protect it all night. I think you will be very surprised to learn where I hold the pollen. Stay tuned to find out.

Was I just talking about eating? Well, if not, I am now.

I eat and eat and eat. Sometimes I feel like all I do is eat. Nectar and pollen, pollen and nectar — that's really all I think about from sunup to sundown.

I have an extremely fast metabolism. My metabolism is what converts my food into energy. I can't leave my nest without a full stomach of nectar. If I did, I would not have enough energy to reach the flowers and get back home. In other words, without a full stomach, I would quickly die from exhaustion.

I'm lucky that plants produce the nectar that gives me energy, and the pollen that provides me with lots of protein.

I cannot survive without nectar and pollen.

It's easy for me to take pollen from a flower because the tiny pollen particles stick to all the hairs on my body.

I take the loosened pollen and stash it in the pollen pockets on my rear legs. The scientific name for my pockets is 'corbicula.' I'm not sure how you pronounce that. People made up the word; we didn't. The pollen pockets are like saddlebags that help me carry all the pollen I have collected back to my nest.

If my pollen pocket is full, it can contain as many as one million pollen grains. I can carry as much as 75% of my body weight in pollen, which means I am very strong for my size. I would compare myself to the Hulk, but I'm not green.

I can't possibly stash ALL the pollen in my pockets. There is always some left on my hairy legs. The pollen stuck to my legs sticks tightly enough that it does not fall off when I fly, but loosely enough to fall off when I land on the next flower.

This process fertilizes the flower and allows it to produce seeds.

This is pollination.

Can you see how bumblebees benefit flowers and how flowers benefit bumblebeees? They are partners in nature because each one benefits the other. That is definitely a win-win situation.

I may be pudgy with five eyes and a pot belly, but don't underestimate how important I am to you. Did you know that if I did not exist, you might not exist? It's true, and it's all about pollination, and I am the pollinating champ.

As I mentioned a short time ago, my hairy legs transfer pollen from one flower or crop to another. This gives the plant the power to produce what it was meant to produce. In other words, when I pollinate a cherry tree, I give the tree the power to produce cherries. I give a peach tree the power to produce peaches, which it cannot do unless pollinated. Get it?

Plants and trees that are grown for food, spices, fibers, beverages, and medicines require pollination. Without pollinators like me, you would not have much to eat, and your world would not have much color.

Pretty impressive for a little insect, right?

(Remember — still NOT a bug.)

Now that you understand pollination, would you like to know the secret behind what makes us the greatest pollinators of all?

The secret is
Buzz Pollination

We bumblebees place our upper bodies close to the inside of the flower. We then grab hold of the pollen-producing part of the plant and beat our wings as fast as we can — remember, up to 200 times a second.

Beating our wings that fast shakes loose a whole lot of pollen. Bumblebees can collect more pollen faster and more efficiently than other pollinators, which is why we are rated
#1!

I also collect nectar, which is my favorite thing to do because nectar is so sweet. It is a liquid that I suck up with my straw-like mouth and my hairy tongue. I store my nectar in my second stomach to carry it back to my nest. There, I regurgitate it for others to eat. I know that sounds really disgusting, but it works for us. (Please don't try this at home.)

As soon as I can return to my nest to drop off the collected pollen and nectar, I head back out to pollinate more flowers. Many, many more flowers. I am as busy as a bee, you know.

I, like all bumblebees, am a homebody. I often fly well over a mile to collect enough pollen and nectar for the day, but, as soon as I do, I head home. I have a great built-in GPS mapping system that guides me.

I have to tell you something about myself — something I find very embarrassing.

I have stinky feet. There, I said it.
Don't laugh. I can't do anything about it.

Bumblebees have an oily film covering their bodies. This film makes us waterproof. That's the good news. The bad news is that the film causes us to have stinky feet.

When I land on a flower, my feet leave my smell on the petals. Other bees smell my odiferous footprints, and they know not to land there. They know that I, or another bee, have already taken the nectar and pollen from the flower.

One good thing about my feet is that they help me find my way back to the entrance to my nest. The stink from my feet acts as a smelly welcome home mat for me.

Let's talk about how you feel about bumblebees. If you hear one buzzing or see a bumblebee flying around your head, do you react like these guys?

I hope not, because I am here to tell you that bumblebees are peaceful. We don't even swarm. We are actually the gentlest of all bees, and we only sting when someone really, really bugs us.

We are so good-natured that getting one of us to sting you is a major undertaking.

Just stand there for a moment. The bumblebee will quickly realize you are not a sweet-smelling daffodil or a pretty little nectar-producing petunia and will fly away. Do not swat at the bee. If you leave it alone, it will leave you alone.

But — if you do NOT show us the respect we deserve, you better believe we will sting you. And, unlike honeybees, which die after they sting once, we can sting over and over and over again without doing any harm to ourselves.

If a bumblebee flies at your face or buzzes around your head, it is trying to give you a warning. You are too close to it or its nest, and you are making the bee very nervous!

If you really annoy one of us to the point where we feel you need stinging, we always respectfully warn you. We stick up a middle leg to let you know we are annoyed by your presence. You might say, we give you the leg, meaning "BACK OFF NOW!"

We can recognize human faces, and we like humans who show us respect. We can build trust with those who are good to us and show us kindness.

Would you want to live in a world without potato chips, french fries, or tater tots? Bumblebees are the only known pollinators of potatoes.

Do you like chocolate? How about strawberries, apples, and nuts? Do you like blueberries, raspberries, watermelon, and cantaloupe? How about peaches, squash, peppers, cucumbers, and tomatoes? All of these are results of pollination. And what would Halloween be without pumpkins and jack-o-lanterns?

Wild animals also rely on bees because their food — nuts, berries, seeds, and fruits — depends on insect pollination.

I also have to take responsibility for the vegetables that you don't seem to like very much even though they are good for you; veggies like broccoli and Brussels sprouts. I'm sorry about those. They weren't my idea.

Okay, it's time for me to admit that we bumblebees are not the only pollinators in the world. Butterflies, moths, beetles, bats, and birds are also pollinators, but, remember, we are the best.

We are also the only pollinators that have the responsibility of collecting enough pollen and nectar to feed all of the members of our colony.

I would be ashamed of myself (maybe), if I did not admit that we are not the best at producing the delicious honey you all like to eat. Honeybees are the best at that. Bumblebees do make honey, but it is not for people. We make just enough honey for ourselves. We make it by chewing pollen and mixing it with our saliva. I guess you could say we spit in our food.

Despite the fact that we bumblebees do not produce much honey, the pollination we provide is worth far more than any amount of honey. Just ask any farmer who makes a living growing alfalfa, red clover, cotton, vegetables, or sunflowers.

So, maybe the next time you see me or another bumblebee, you'll say 'thank you' instead of **'Get away from me!'**

You might also want to be nice to me when I tell you that I live for only 28 days.

Now that you know lots about me and how important I am to your life, I want you to be aware of something.

Bee populations are declining at an extremely fast rate. Bumblebees are listed as endangered.

Why should you care if bumblebees go extinct?

Because, if bees die off, it will end most life.

You need us.
And now, we need you.

Threats to Bumblebees

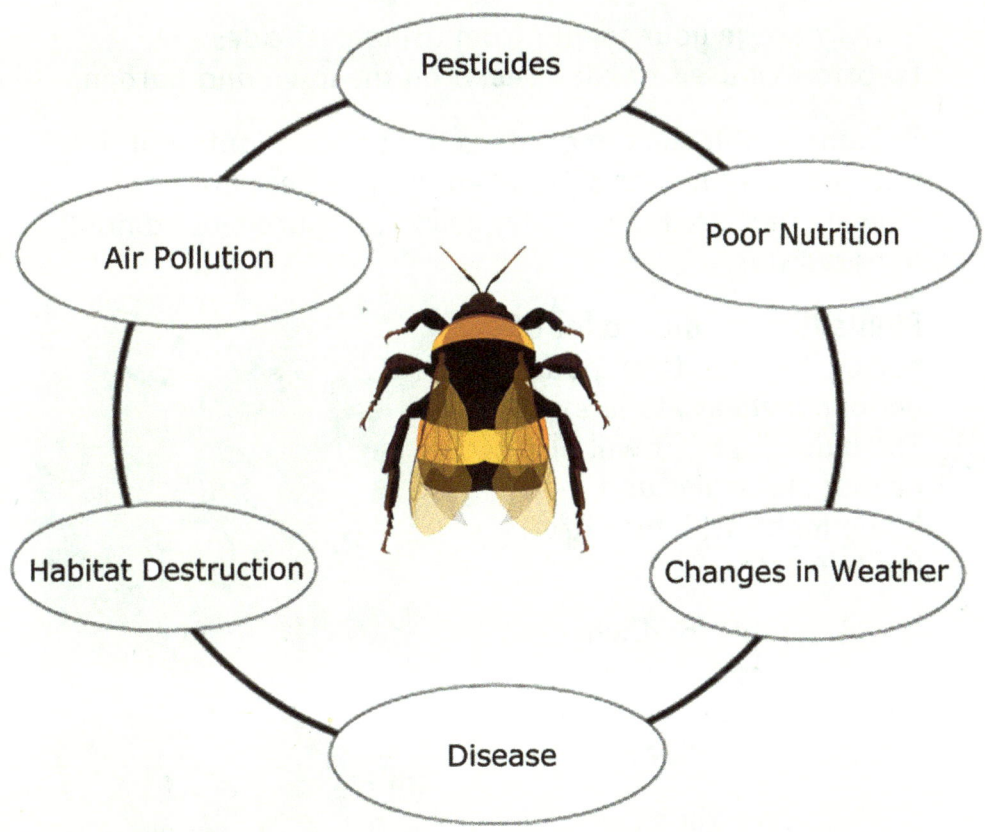

Since a large part of the decline of bees is being caused by humans, it can also be reversed by humans; humans like you.

Do you want to help keep the bumblebees in your area healthy?

Please say yes.

There are lots of ways you can help bumblebees.

1. Provide nesting sites for us by leaving some parts of your yard a little wild. Don't mow or rake there.

2. Discourage your family from using pesticides (substances used to kill insects) on the lawn and garden.

3. Plant wildflowers in gardens or in pots. Plant anything that produces nectar and pollen. Bumblebees are not fussy. Flowers that are blue, white, yellow, or purple are among our favorites.

Plants that produce a lot of nectar, like a butterfly bush, get bumblebees really excited. The butterfly bush will also attract butterflies and hummingbirds, which are fun to watch.

4. Eat organic food whenever possible because organic foods are grown without the use of pesticides.

5. Don't ever kill a bumblebee. Just walk away. If you see a friend kill or harm one of us, POLITELY explain why that is wrong to do.

6. And, please, never disturb a bumblebee nest.

If you would do some of these things to help me and other bumblebees, it would BEE amazing!

Thank you.

www.ingramcontent.com/pod-product-compliance
Lightning Source LLC
Chambersburg PA
CBHW081413160426

42811CB00096B/794